ONE NATION FOR ALL
IMMIGRANTS IN THE UNITED STATES

LIFE AS A NIGERIAN AMERICAN

VIC KOVACS

PowerKiDS
press.

Published in 2018 by The Rosen Publishing Group, Inc.
29 East 21st Street, New York, NY 10010

Cataloging-in-Publication Data
Names: Kovacs, Vic.
Title: Life as a Nigerian American / Vic Kovacs.
Description: New York : PowerKids Press, 2018. | Series: One nation for all: immigrants in the United States | Includes index.
Identifiers: LCCN ISBN 9781538323366 (pbk.) | ISBN 9781538322406 (library bound) | ISBN 9781538323373 (6 pack)
Subjects: LCSH: Immigrants--United States--Juvenile literature. | Nigerian Americans.
Classification: LCC E184.N55 K68 2018 | DDC 973'.049669--dc23

Developed and produced for Rosen by BlueApple*Works* Inc.
Art Director: T.J. Choleva
Managing Editor for BlueApple*Works*: Melissa McClellan
Designer: Joshua Avramson
Photo Research: Jane Reid
Editor: Marcia Abramson

Photo Credits: Cover Jordi C/Shutterstock.com; title page Sean Pavone/Shutterstock.com; flag Les Cunliffe/Dreamstime; background HorenkO/Shutterstock; p. 4 AS photo studio/Shutterstock; p. 6 Chima222/Creative Commons; p. 8 Serban Bogdan/Shutterstock; p. 10 Public Domain; p. 12 Shiraz Chakera/Creative Commons; p. 13 Kamira/Shutterstock; p. 14 Jordi C/Shutterstock.com; p. 16 Colin Underhill/Alamy Stock Photo; p. 18 Mila Supinskaya Glashchenko/Shutterstock; p. 20 Richard Levine/Alamy Stock Photo; p. 22 karelnoppe/Shutterstock; p. 24 Frances Roberts/Alamy Stock Photo; p. 26 Jerry Coli/Dreamstime.com; p. 29 Public Domain

Manufactured in the United States of America
CPSIA Compliance Information: Batch BW18PK: For Further Information contact
Rosen Publishing, New York, New York at 1-800-237-9932.

CONTENTS

U.S. families with roots in the country of Nigeria are known as Nigerian Americans.

WHO ARE NIGERIAN AMERICANS?

Nigerian Americans are the largest group of African **immigrants** currently in America. They are also one of the most highly educated **ethnic groups** in the country. Some are American born and come from families that have been in America for **generations**. Others continue to arrive and build lives for themselves today.

Often coming to America to further their education, many Nigerians remain after graduation and become hardworking Americans. Many have children who are raised with both American and Nigerian **culture**.

These cultures are varied. Nigeria is made up of many different ethnic groups, including the Igbo, Yoruba, and Hausa peoples.

Traditional Nigerian dress varies by region, but bright colors are everywhere. Men and women usually wear a cap or headdress.

Nigerian Americans speak a number of languages, including English, and practice a variety of religions, such as Christianity, Islam, and more.

Nigerian Americans have made up a diverse, vibrant portion of the American population for many years. Today, more than 210,000 people born in Nigeria live in the United States along with more than 160,000 of their American-born children.

One Country, Many Peoples

Nigeria has the largest population of any country in Africa. That population is made up of several different ethnic groups of people. Each group has its own unique history, traditions, and culture. Here are some of the largest:

Hausa: The Hausa people are mostly located in the northern part of Nigeria. Historically they have mostly been farmers, growing crops and raising livestock. Most Hausa are **Muslims**, and they are the largest ethnic group in the country. They are sometimes grouped together with the Fulani people. The two groups originally spoke different languages, but today, many Fulani speak Hausa. Marriage between the groups is also common. Together, the Hausa-Fulani people make up about 29 percent of Nigeria's population.

Yoruba: The Yoruba people follow a number of different religions, including Christianity, Islam, and more traditional faiths practiced by their ancestors. Yoruba are the second largest ethnic group in Nigeria, making up about 21 percent of the population.

Igbo: The Igbo people live in many smaller groups that are geographically spread out. Their language, also called Igbo, contains many dialects that differ based on location. They are mostly Christian, which sometimes leads to conflict with Muslim ethnic groups. Today, they are known in Nigeria for being an important part of the nation's oil business. They make up about 18 percent of the country's population.

In total, there are over 500 ethnic groups in the country, with at least as many languages!

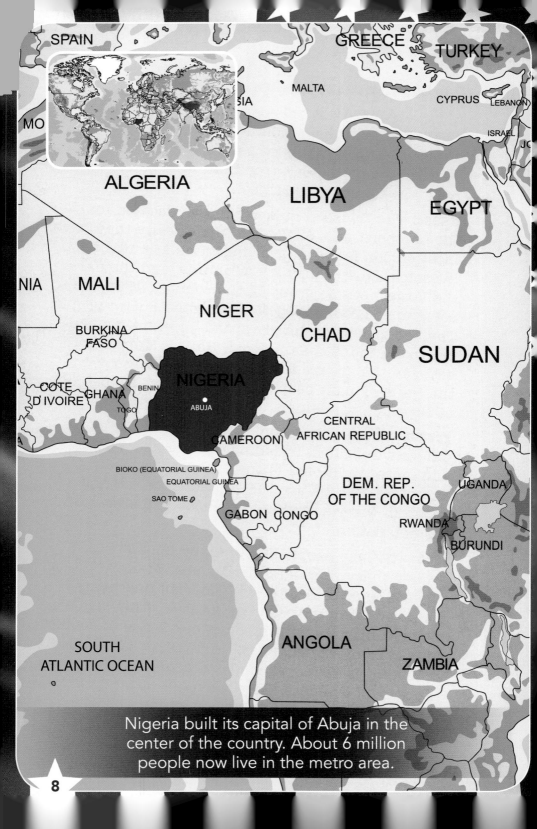

Nigeria built its capital of Abuja in the center of the country. About 6 million people now live in the metro area.

HISTORY OF NIGERIA

Nigeria is a country on the west side of Africa. It is bordered by the countries of Benin to the west, Niger to the north, Chad to the northeast, and Cameroon to the east. To the south is the Gulf of Guinea, part of the South Atlantic Ocean. It is the most populous country in all of Africa, with over 180 million people! That's a little over half of the population of the United States, all in a country that's just a third bigger than the state of Texas, or twice the size of California. As you might imagine, that makes it a little bit more crowded than America!

The area that today is known as Nigeria has been occupied by human beings for a very long time. The earliest evidence of civilizations in Nigeria dates all the way back to the fifth century BC. Statues dating to that time have been found in a village called Nok. As a result, these first known tribes are called the Nok people.

Many indigenous people in what is now Nigeria were kidnapped and sold as slaves during the slave trade.

Starting more than a **millennium** later, early city-states and kingdoms began to spring up. Many of these relied on trade with other regions to support themselves. One of the most important of these early states was called Kanem-Bornu. It was originally located just outside of modern-day Nigeria. However, by the eleventh century, the heads of the state had all adopted the Islamic faith. They began to expand their empire south into what we now know as Nigeria.

The first Europeans to come to Nigeria were Portuguese navigators in the late fifteenth century. They were followed by the British, French, and Dutch. This led to one of the most tragic chapters in Nigerian history: the slave trade. Over the next few hundred years, millions of people were forcibly taken from their homes and families and sold into slavery. These were also the first Nigerians brought to America. However, because they had no choice whatsoever in the matter, they are not generally considered immigrants.

Starting in the early nineteenth century, Britain began to take more of an interest in what would eventually become Nigeria. This was a time of war for many of the different ethnic groups and states, and the British were able to defeat many of the locals and establish their own rule. They outlawed the slave trade and governed through indirect rule. This meant that the British placed traditional, local rulers who were friendly to them in charge.

At the turn of the twentieth century, the two main British colonies in the area, Lagos and the Southern Nigeria Protectorate, were united as the Colony of Nigeria. In 1914, the Colony of Nigeria combined with the Northern Nigeria Protectorate to form the Colony and Protectorate of Nigeria.

Abuja, built in the 1980s, was inspired by beautiful capitals like Paris and Washington, D.C.

The Colony and Protectorate of Nigeria became an official member of the British Commonwealth, a collection of countries and colonies around the world all ruled by the **British Crown**. Other members include Canada, Australia, and at the time, India.

Throughout the first half of the twentieth century, a number of government reforms moved Nigeria closer to self-governance and further away from British rule. This all culminated in 1960, when Nigeria achieved its independence from Britain. Nigeria was now free to decide its own destiny, but it was not always a peaceful journey.

Lady Liberty

In the early part of the twentieth century, many immigrants' first sight of their new home was the Statue of Liberty on Liberty Island. Boats bringing immigrants to America would pass her by on their way to Ellis Island. Once at Ellis Island, the ships would dock, and their passengers would disembark to be processed into their new country.

Designed by the French sculptor Frederic Auguste Bartholdi, it was actually built by Gustave Eiffel, who would become famous for designing the Eiffel Tower in Paris. It is made of copper and was originally the color of dull pennies. It got its distinctive green color through a process called oxidization caused by the statue's constant exposure to seawater.

Today, Lady Liberty, as she is also known, is a popular tourist attraction. However, since her dedication in 1886, she has remained a powerful symbol welcoming new Americans to the freedom they can enjoy in their new home. As the poem at her base reads, "Give me your tired, your poor, your huddled masses yearning to break free."

More Nigerian families live in the United States than anywhere else outside Nigeria. Nigerian Americans make up 0.6 percent of the U.S. population.

Nigeria's modern history, since its beginning as an independent country in 1960, has been rocky. It has been marked by political unrest and **civil war**. The majority of the population in Nigeria is based in its northern regions. This has led many people in other areas of the country to feel like they aren't being represented in the various governments that have held power. These problems are often made worse by ethnic and historical differences. Some groups have tried to seize power and solve these issues through force. For example, in 1966 there was a **military coup** led mostly by Igbo officers from the eastern part of the country. This led to a counter-coup, a period of military rule, and a civil war. A new constitution was finally drafted in 1978. This pattern of military rule, replaced by civilian rule, only to be replaced again by the military, would continue until 1999.

Periods of unrest like this often lead to immigration. People may feel unsafe, or they may believe they're not being offered the same opportunities that others are.

One of the main reasons Nigerians immigrate to America is education. Education has long been an important value in Nigerian society. It is viewed as both a way to increase one's economic status and as something that leads to greater happiness and fulfillment as a person.

The value of education was even expressed by the Nigerian government. The Biafra war was a civil war that took place between 1967 and 1970. Afterwards, Nigeria became more stable and prosperous, and sponsored a number of scholarships for students hoping to attend college. Many of these students applied to, and were accepted by, American schools. This trend has continued to the present day, with many of the best schools in the country reporting large numbers of Nigerian students. Some examples include Harvard, Yale, and Columbia. Today, many of these students are either new immigrants or the children of immigrants.

This focus on education has led to an interesting fact: today, Nigerians are one of the most highly educated ethnic groups in all of America. About 40 percent of Nigerian Americans hold at least a bachelor's degree.

One thing that helps many Nigerian immigrants live happily in American society is their knowledge of English, which is the official language of Nigeria.

Today, Nigerians live all over America. They live in large population centers, such as New York City, Chicago, and Los Angeles, as well as smaller cities like Columbus, Ohio, and Newark, New Jersey. The state with the largest Nigerian population is Texas.

The more than 370,000 Nigerian Americans in the United States are the largest group from any one African country. For many immigrants, America was seen as a place they could receive a great education and put their skills to use in whatever field they chose. The number of Nigerian success stories has shown this to be true.

Many Nigerian Americans, especially younger ones, wear Western clothing in their daily lives. They may wear traditional Nigerian clothes for special events like weddings.

LIVING AS AMERICANS

Nigerian immigrants have found much success in America, but it's not always easy. Coming to a new country is difficult no matter where you're from. Integrating into a new culture can take time. Many immigrants try to find a balance between the culture they're from, and the culture they're entering. Nigerian immigrants are unique because there are so many different cultures in their homeland. There's no one particular type of Nigerian culture, but rather a number of different ethnic and geographic traditions. Nigerians bring a number of things to American culture, but they also have some unique hurdles to overcome once they're here.

Many Nigerian immigrants are well-educated when they arrive in the United States. Many continue their educations once they move to their new home. About a third of Nigerian immigrants go on to earn at least one advanced degree.

Marchers wear green and white,
the colors of Nigeria's flag,
for a National Day parade in New York.

English, as the official government language of Nigeria, is spoken fluently by many immigrants when they arrive in America. Being able to communicate allows immigrants to enter the job market more easily. It also helps with more basic things like making friends and navigating their new home.

★ **Making friends:** Because Nigerians have been immigrating to America for decades, there are established communities in many cities.

This gives new immigrants a place they can start their new life that feels a little bit like home. It also gives them access to people who have been where they've been and can offer advice. Some of the largest Nigerian communities are in Houston, New York City, Washington, D.C. and its surrounding areas, and Chicago.

★ Faith: Faith is another way Nigerian immigrants can find a sense of community. The majority of immigrants practice Christianity, at 70 percent, with the next largest group being Muslims. This means that they're often able to find places to worship and people who share their faith and values.

★ Holidays: Many of the holidays celebrated by Nigerians are also celebrated by other Americans. These include Easter and Christmas for Christians, and the end of **Ramadan** for Muslims. One holiday that is unique for Nigerians in National Day, also known as Nigerian Independence Day, on October 1. It celebrates the day Nigeria achieved its independence from Britain. In some communities, the celebration lasts an entire week!

★ Family life: Although weddings in America generally follow the customs of whatever religious group is hosting them, Nigerian traditions are often incorporated. These include traditional food, dress, music, and dance.

Many Nigerian immigrants see their children who are born or raised in America go on to great success.

Nigerian Proverbs

Like most peoples around the world, the various groups that make up Nigeria have unique phrases that illustrate lessons and teach wisdom, known as proverbs. Here are just a few. Can you figure out their meaning?

"Death does not recognize a king."

"An elephant is a hare in another town."

"A child who is carried on the back will not know how far the journey is."

"When you are eating with the devil you must use a long spoon."

"No matter how dark it is, the hand always knows the way to the mouth."

As in many cultures, Nigerian families want to see their children do well in school. Nigerian American children are encouraged to get good grades and to value education. Many Nigerian Americans go to Ivy League Schools like Harvard and Yale when they are older. Young Nigerian Americans are often encouraged to go into careers with clear goals and benefits.

Nigeria Day celebrations often include vendors selling traditional dishes at "chop bars."

★ **Food:** It's impossible to pinpoint one **iconic** Nigerian dish due to the large number of cultures. However, one thing that many Nigerian cuisines have in common? They can be VERY spicy. Nigerian food is slowly becoming more popular in the United States. This is especially true in cities with large Nigerian populations like Houston.

Nigeria has so many different ethnic groups that the food varies all over the country. Here are some dishes that have become known as national favorites:

Dodo: Fried plantains (a relative of bananas, but not sweet)

Ewa Agoyin: Smashed beans cooked in a hot sauce

Suya: A spicy beef, lamb, or chicken kebab, often served in a newspaper wrapper

Banga: A peppery soup cooked with fish and palm fruits

Kuli-kuli: Snack balls made from roasted peanuts, peanut oil, onions, salt, and cayenne pepper

Akara: Fried patties made from ground black-eye peas, onion, tomatoes, eggs, and chili peppers

Puff-puff: Fried dough balls, often sprinkled with sugar

★ **Challenges:** One thing that many Nigerian immigrants find themselves facing is **prejudice**. Racism is an ongoing issue in the United States today. Some Americans may have preconceived ideas about what Nigerians are like, and these ideas are often wrong and hurtful. Organizations like the Nigerian American Foundation work to protect Nigerian Americans from discrimination and to empower this community economically, socially, and politically.

Hakeem Abdul Olajuwon, a Nigerian American, is one of the greatest players in the history of the NBA. The seven-foot center played from 1984 to 2002 for Houston and Toronto.

AMAZING ACHIEVEMENTS

Nigerian Americans, both first-generation immigrants and their descendants, have had a huge impact on American society. Here are a few well-known Nigerian Americans:

★ Andre Iguodala: The basketball star won a National Basketball Association (NBA) championship with Golden State in 2015 and an Olympic gold medal with Team USA in 2012. His father is a Nigerian American and he was born in Illinois.

★ Chamillionaire: Born Hakeem Seriki, Chamillionaire was raised in Houston. A successful rapper and musician, he's probably best known for his single "Ridin'." He won a Grammy for it in 2007.

★ Donald Faison: An actor, he's probably best known for roles in the film *Clueless*, the cartoon *Clone High*, and for starring as Turk in the long-running sitcom *Scrubs*.

★ **Dr. Bennet Omalu:** A Nigerian-born pathologist, he brought to light a serious condition caused by head injuries among football players. His story was told in the 2015 movie *Concussion*. He now lives in California, where he is a chief medical examiner and a college professor.

★ **Adeparo Oduye:** An award-winning actress, she's probably best known for her role in *12 Years a Slave*, which won the Best Picture Oscar in 2014.

★ **Adaora Udoji:** An American journalist of Nigerian descent. She has worked for CNN, ABC News, and Court TV, among others. She has covered important news events such as Hurricane Katrina, the Iraq and Afghanistan wars, as well as lighter subjects like the Tour de France.

★ **Victor Ukpolo:** Considered the first Nigerian-born person to run an American university. Ukpolo was the chancellor of Southern University at New Orleans. He rose to national prominence after Hurricane Katrina. Ukpolo led efforts to repair his school's campus, which had been badly damaged by the hurricane. He successfully raised millions of dollars to restore his campus.

Nigerian American writer Chimamanda Ngozi Adichie (in red dress) gives back to her native country by teaching creative writing to students like these in Abuja.

★ Chimamanda Ngozi Adichie: One of the most acclaimed writers working today. She was awarded the prestigious MacArthur Fellowship in 2008. Adichie writes both fiction, including short stories and novels, as well as incredibly popular nonfiction. One of her most popular books is 2014's *We Should All Be Feminists*. She has also received an O. Henry Prize, one of short fiction's top awards.

These are just a few of the many, many Nigerian Americans who excel in every field. Their hard work makes the United States and the world a better place. What amazing things will the next generation of Nigerian Americans accomplish?

Glossary

British Crown The state that oversees British territories, with the current British monarch as its head.

civil war A conflict in which two groups from the same country engage in hostilities.

culture A collection of shared stories and other traditions that bind a group together.

ethnic group A group of people who share a culture.

generation A group of people who are all born within a certain number of years of each other. For example, parents are of one generation, and their children are of another.

iconic Symbolic

immigrant Someone who comes to live in a new country.

military coup An event in which a country's military overthrows the current government.

millennium One thousand years.

Muslim Someone who believes in the religion Islam, which follows the prophet Muhammad.

prejudice A negative assumption about a group of people that is not based in fact.

Ramadan A month of religious fasting observed by Muslims.

For More Information

Further Reading

Meister, Cari. *Meals in Nigeria.*
Minneapolis, MN: Jump!, 2017.

Onyefulu, Ifeoma. *The Girl Who Married a Ghost: and Other Tales from Nigeria.*
London, UK: Frances Lincoln Children's Books, 2010.

Rau, Dana Meachen. *It's Cool to Learn About Countries: Nigeria.* North Mankato, MN: Cherry Lake Publishing, 2010.

Seavey, Lura Rogers. *Nigeria.*
New York: Scholastic, 2016.

Websites

Due to the changing nature of Internet links, PowerKids Press has developed an online list of websites related to the subject of this book. This site is updated regularly. Please use this link to access the list:
www.powerkidslinks.com/cs/nigerianam

Index